AF380022

The ABC of you and me

sj Molver

Aa is for Abraham
who has one arm.

Abraham was born with his right arm ending just above the elbow. He says it doesn't bother him and he loves to write, paint and play basketball.

Aa

Bb is for Betina who is partially **blind**.

She's learning to use a guide cane which will help her find obstacles in front of her, such as steps and pavements. Betina loves music and is learning to play the piano.

Bb

Cc is for Colin
who cooks.

Colin's mother owns a bakery and
for as long as he can remember,
he's been helping her bake
and cook cakes, pies and other
scrumptious things to eat. Colin
hopes to be a chef one day.

Cc

Dd is for Doloris who is deaf.

Doloris cannot hear. She speaks using sign language and can also read lips. She loves bright colours and can "listen" to music through vibrations. Doloris plays chess and collects buttons which she keeps in a jar beside her bed.

Dd

Ee is for Enok who has **epilepsy**.

Epilepsy is a condition that affects the brain, causing seizures. A seizure can cause lots of things to happen all at once. This is scary for Enok but with the right medication he can manage his epilepsy.

Ee

Ff is for Florence who floats.

Florence is a daydreamer. She believes in magic and often wonders what it would be like to float, high up above the clouds to the very top of the world and beyond. Do you believe in magic?

Ff

Gg is for Gus who wears glasses.

Everyone's eyes are different; some people need to wear glasses to see more clearly. Gus is very proud of his new glasses. Aren't they lovely?

Gg

Hh is for Harriet with all that **hair**.

Harriet has the most fabulously - wild hair. She absolutely loves it and so do I.

Hh

Ii is for Isaac who itches.

Isaac sometimes suffers with itchy skin, also know as eczema. Isaac's mum has special cream at home to help make him feel better and calm the itchiness.

Ii

Jj is for Juliana who jumps.

Juliana loves jumping, she even practises it in her sleep! She hopes to one day jump high enough to touch the stars. How high can you jump?

Jj
burp

Kk is for Kyle who is kind.

Kyle is such a kind, sweet boy. He received a special mention from his teacher this week for being a kind friend in class. Have you done something kind today?

Kk

Ll is for Lina who has **learning difficulties**.

Lina finds it hard to communicate and needs lots of help understanding new things. If you meet her, be sure to be kind and patient. Lina loves rainbows and unicorns, they always make her smile.

L l

Mm is for Marc who runs marathons.

Marc is committed to running, he just loves it and has even run a marathon. That's 352 football fields – that's a lot of running. He wants to run more marathons and by doing this, he is hoping to raise some money for charity. Go Marc!

Mm

Nn is for Nandi who doesn't like noise.

Nandi is extremely sensitive to different sounds and this can be distressing for her. Nandi's mum bought her a pair of headphones that block out noise. She is much happier now. Are there any sounds that you don't like?

Nn

Oo is for Oskar who is overwhelmed.

Oskar often feels overwhelmed. This means that he feels a lot of emotions all at once and has to take time to calm and reset himself. I think we can all feel overwhelmed at times.

Oo

Pp is for Penelope who has a **prosthetic leg**.

Penelope lost her leg in an accident when she was very small so some clever doctors made her a new one. This is called a prosthetic. Penelope has to have it adjusted every so often because she is still growing. She enjoys swimming, telling stories and writing in her secret diary. She's also really good at hopping.

P p

Qq is for Quinn who likes quiet time.

Quinn enjoys spending time on his own. He listens to the birdsong, feels the warm breeze in his hair and the sun on his face. Quinn is mindful of his surroundings.

Qq

Rr is for Ruby who loves reading.

Ruby belongs to the worlds which live within the pages of the books she reads. Sometimes she's solving mysteries and sometimes she's lost in faraway realms filled with enchantment and magical friends. What kind of worlds do you love reading about?

Rr

Ss is for Solomon who likes wearing skirts.

Solomon loves dressing up: sometimes he's a pirate, sometimes he's a doctor but mostly he loves dressing up as a girl and he especially loves wearing skirts. What's your favourite thing to dress up in?

Ss

Tt is for Tina who is having treatment.

Tina is having treatment for cancer. Treatment is a course of medication that you take over a certain amount of time. Sometimes your hair falls out. This can be scary but when it's over, your hair will grow back again. Tina is almost finished with her treatment. She has been extremely brave.

Tt
GET
WELL
SOON

Uu is for Umar who rides a unicycle.

I know Umar who rides his unicycle to school every morning. He's incredibly good at it and perhaps if you see him, you could ask him to teach you how to ride just like him.

Uu

Vv is for Violet who has vitiligo.

This means that her skin loses its pigment cells and she has patches of different coloured skin on her face and hands. She used to be shy about it but now she loves that she's different. Violet grows vegetables and flowers and would love to be a botanist one day.

Vv

Ww is for William who uses a wheelchair.

William has Perthes Disease. This is where his hip needs time to heal after being misshapen from blood vessels not forming properly. Sometimes William uses a wheelchair to take pressure off his bones while they grow and recover. People use wheelchairs for lots of different reasons. Do you know anyone who uses one?

Ww

Xx is for Xandri who needs an x-ray.

Xandri fell out of a tree while playing hide and seek and now she needs an x-ray because her arm hurts. An x-ray is when the doctor takes a photo of the inside of your body to see if any bones are broken. This can be scary and sometimes uncomfortable but it's important to stay nice and still. Have you ever had an x-ray?

Xx

Yy is for Yusuf who yells.

Yusuf yells and cries a lot. Perhaps it's because he is feeling scared, frustrated or left out. Yusuf's mother has asked the doctors for help because she wants to make him feel better. Asking for help can be hard but people are here to help when you are ready.

Yy

Zz is for Zara who
is just, well, **zany**.

Zara is fun, wild and friendly. She
loves dressing up, making friends
and trying new things. She's fearless
and quirky and her friends all call
her "zany-Zara". Perhaps there's a
little of Zara in all of us.

Zz

Although we are all
different, we
all deserve to be loved
equally.

sj Molver ♡
x

As well as writing and drawing, SJ Molver enjoys hiking, foraging and stargazing. She lives in Scotland with her family, including three suspicious hens and a cat called Simon.
Peck peck
waaak
bok bok

This book is for anyone who has ever felt a little out of place. You are not alone and you are loved.

SJ Molver

www.sjmolver.com